"Beautiful, simple and wonderful. Children are helped to see who Jesus really is."

JON GEMMELL, The Proclamation Trust Blog, July 2017

"This book is a must for children, parents, grandparents, godparents and Sunday school teachers. And if you're none of these, then still buy it! I love it."

JANE WATKINS, Growing Young Disciples

"It was no surprise to find "The Storm that Stopped" gripped my children. The narrative and the illustrations combine to help my children feel the disciples' wildly changing emotions through the story. We felt the storm! My children love the visual scales measuring the impact of the storm. I love the final pages which excellently and simply help us understand that this story has a clear purpose in showing us who Jesus Christ is. Thank you!"

ED DREW, Director, Faith in Kids

"Jesus had finished teaching the crowd, and now he had something to teach his friends - but they didn't know it yet..." Alison Mitchell has cleverly retold Mark's account of Jesus calming the storm, focusing readers on what Jesus had taught his own disciples - he does what only God can do. "The Storm That Stopped" is a great addition to every child's must-have list."

SANDY GALEA, MBM Children's Minister, Rooty Hill Anglican, Sydney

"One of the most creative children's books we've seen."

IDEA MAGAZINE, July 2016

thegoodbook
for children

The Storm that Stopped
© Catalina Echeverri / The Good Book Company 2015.
Reprinted 2016, 2017, 2018 (twice), 2019, 2020, 2021, 2022.

Illustrated by Catalina Echeverri | Design & Art Direction by André Parker

'The Good Book For Children' is an imprint of The Good Book Company Ltd

thegoodbook.co.uk | thegoodbook.com | thegoodbook.com.au | thegoodbook.co.nz | thegoodbook.co.in

ISBN: 9781910307960 | Printed in India

THE STORM THAT

WRITTEN BY
ALISON
MITCHELL

illustrated by
CATALINA
ECHEVERRI

STOPPED

A TRUE STORY ABOUT WHO JESUS really IS

One day, long ago,
Jesus was teaching people by the sea.

Soon, some more people arrived.

Then others. Then more, AND MORE –

until there were people

EVERYWHERE

The crowds were just too big!

No one could see Jesus and no one could hear Jesus.

So Jesus asked his friends, the disciples,
to push their boat out onto the water.

He sat in the boat and the huge crowd
spread out along the beach.
Now, they could all see and hear Jesus
as he told them all about God.

When he finished teaching the people,
Jesus said to his friends:

LET'S GO OVER TO THE OTHER SIDE OF THE SEA.

Jesus had finished teaching the crowd, and now he had something to teach his friends

- but they didn't Know it yet...

So they all jumped in the boat with him and set sail across the sea...

Jesus was so tired - he'd been
teaching the people all day -
so he lay down in the back of the boat
and fell fast asleep.

It was a quiet evening.
 The water gently lapped against the boat,
and the sun slowly set in the sky.

Jesus was sleeping.
 The disciples were quietly talking.
  Then all of a sudden...

They were in the middle of the biggest, loudest, scariest, most GINORMOUS storm you could imagine!

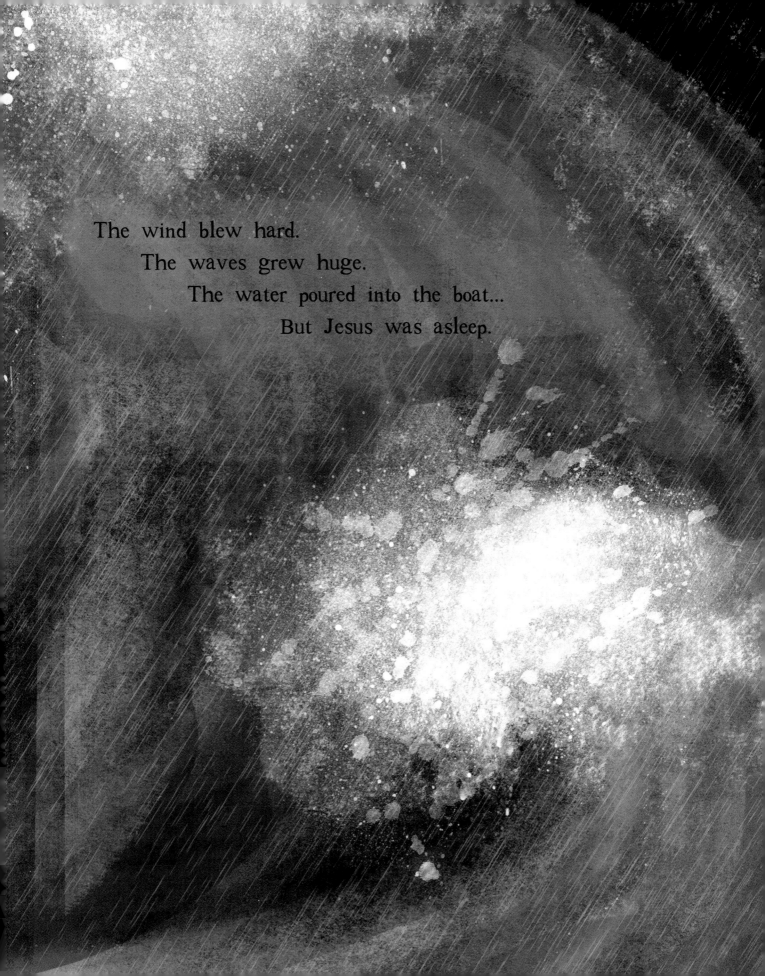

The wind blew hard.
The waves grew huge.
The water poured into the boat...
But Jesus was asleep.

DON'T YOU CARE?

What a silly thing to say to Jesus!
Of course he cared.
He loved his friends so much that one
day he was going to die for them.

Jesus stood up in the boat.
The wind was still blowing.

The waves were
bigger than ever.

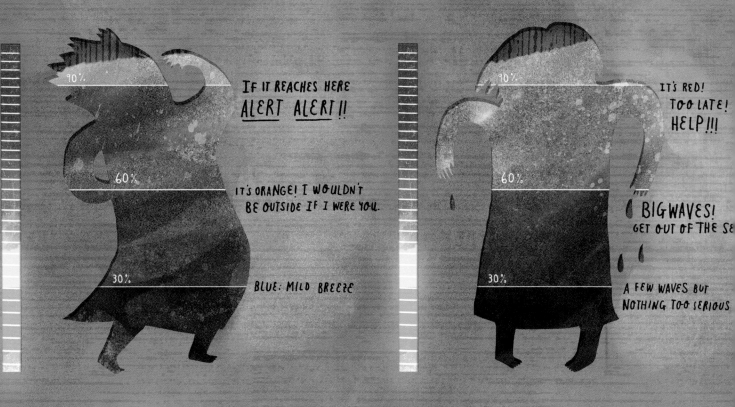

The water was pouring into the boat quicker than the disciples could tip it out again...

The boat was sinking!

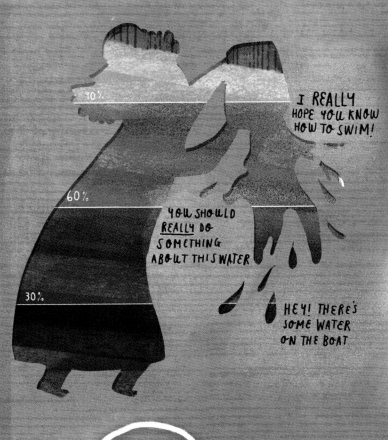

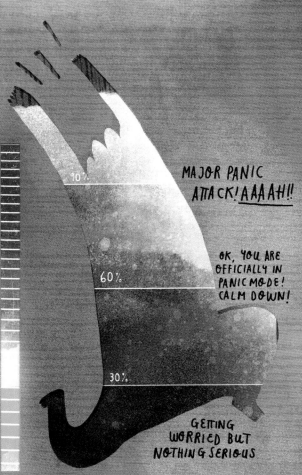

But then Jesus did something amazing.

He didn't help his friends pour the
water out of the boat. He didn't help
them try to row back to land.

Jesus simply SPOKE.
But he didn't speak to the disciples.
He spoke to the storm.
To the wind. And to the waves.

Just three little words
...and the storm stopped.

Right away, at that very moment,
the sea was quiet, still and calm.

Then Jesus looked at his friends.

WHY ARE YOU SO AFRAID? DO YOU STILL NOT TRUST ME?

But they were terrified.
And they asked each other:

This is what Jesus
wanted to teach them.
He wanted them to
Know who he really is.

The disciples already Knew a lot
about God from his special book.
They Knew that God made
EVERYTHING.

He made the world.
He made the sun and the
moon and the stars.

GO

And he made the sea
and the wind as well.

D

They knew that only God can tell
the sea what to do. That only God
can tell the wind when to blow or
the waves when to crash.

Only God can do these things.

But the disciples had just
seen Jesus do the same
things God can do!

So what is the answer
to their question?
Who is Jesus?

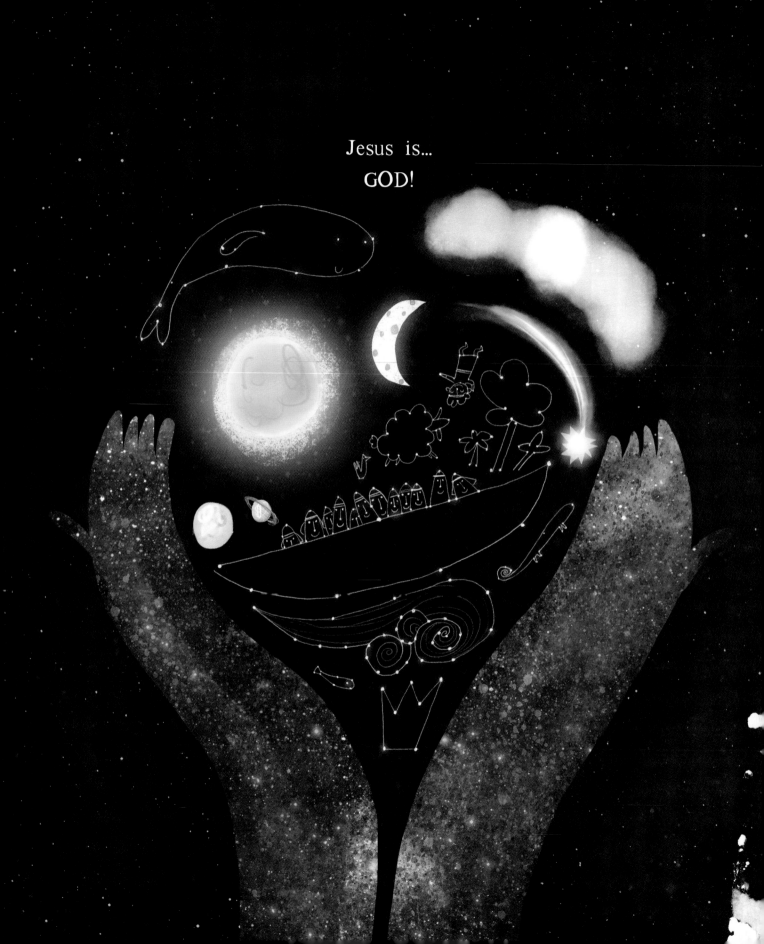

Jesus is...
GOD!

HOW DO WE KNOW
ABOUT THE STORM THAT STOPPED?

The account of Jesus calming the storm was written
down for us by Mark (a friend of Jesus' disciple, Peter)
in the New Testament part of the Bible.

You will find it in Mark 4 v 35-41.

At the end of this true story, the disciples ask each other:
"Who is this? Even the wind and the waves obey him!"
The rest of Mark's book shows us the answer to their question.
Jesus is able to do things that only God can do (for example, in
Psalm 107 v 23-32 it is God who saves some sailors by calming
a storm). So, who is Jesus? He is the Son of God!

Enjoy all of the award-winning "Tales That Tell The Truth" series: